Understanding My Emotions

When I'm Lonely

Understanding My Emotions

When I'm Angry
When I'm Embarrassed
When I'm Happy
When I'm Lonely
When I'm Overwhelmed
When I'm Sad
When I'm Scared
When I'm Sorry
When I'm Surprised
When I'm Worried

Understanding My Emotions

When I'm Lonely

ALEXANDRA DALTON

**Understanding My Emotions
When I'm Lonely**

Copyright © 2016 by Village Earth Press, a division of Harding House Publishing. All rights reserved. No part of this publication may be reproduced or transmitted in any form or by any means, electronic or mechanical, including photocopying, recording, taping, or any information storage and retrieval system, without permission from the publisher.

Village Earth Press
Vestal, New York 13850
www.villageearthpress.com

First Printing
9 8 7 6 5 4 3 2 1

Series ISBN (paperback): 978-1-62524-440-6
ISBN (paperback): 978-1-62524-379-9
ebook ISBN: 978-1-62524-135-1
   Library of Congress Control Number: 2014944103

Author: Dalton, Alexandra.

Contents

To the Teacher	7
When I'm Lonely	8
Find Out More	42
Feeling Words	44
Index	46
Picture Credits	47
About the Author	48

To the Teacher

More than a hundred years ago, John Dewey insisted that the true purpose of schooling was not simply to teach children a trade but to train them in deeper habits of mind. Social-emotional learning builds on Dewey's theory further, suggesting that emotional skills are crucial to both academic performance and future success in life.

The research is definitive: emotional training is good for children! A recent study, reported in the *New York Times*, found that preschoolers who had even a single year of social-emotional training continued to perform better two years after they left the program; they were less aggressive and less anxious than children who hadn't participated in the program. Another study found that K-12 students who received some form of emotional instruction scored an average of 11 percentile points higher on standardized achievement tests. A similar study found a nearly 20 percent decrease in students' violent behaviors.

The goal of this series of books, UNDERSTANDING MY EMOTIONS, is to instill in young children a foundation of emotional intelligence. Use these books to help your students learn to understand, identify, and regulate their emotions. Give them important tools that will serve them well for the rest of their lives!

When I'm LONELY

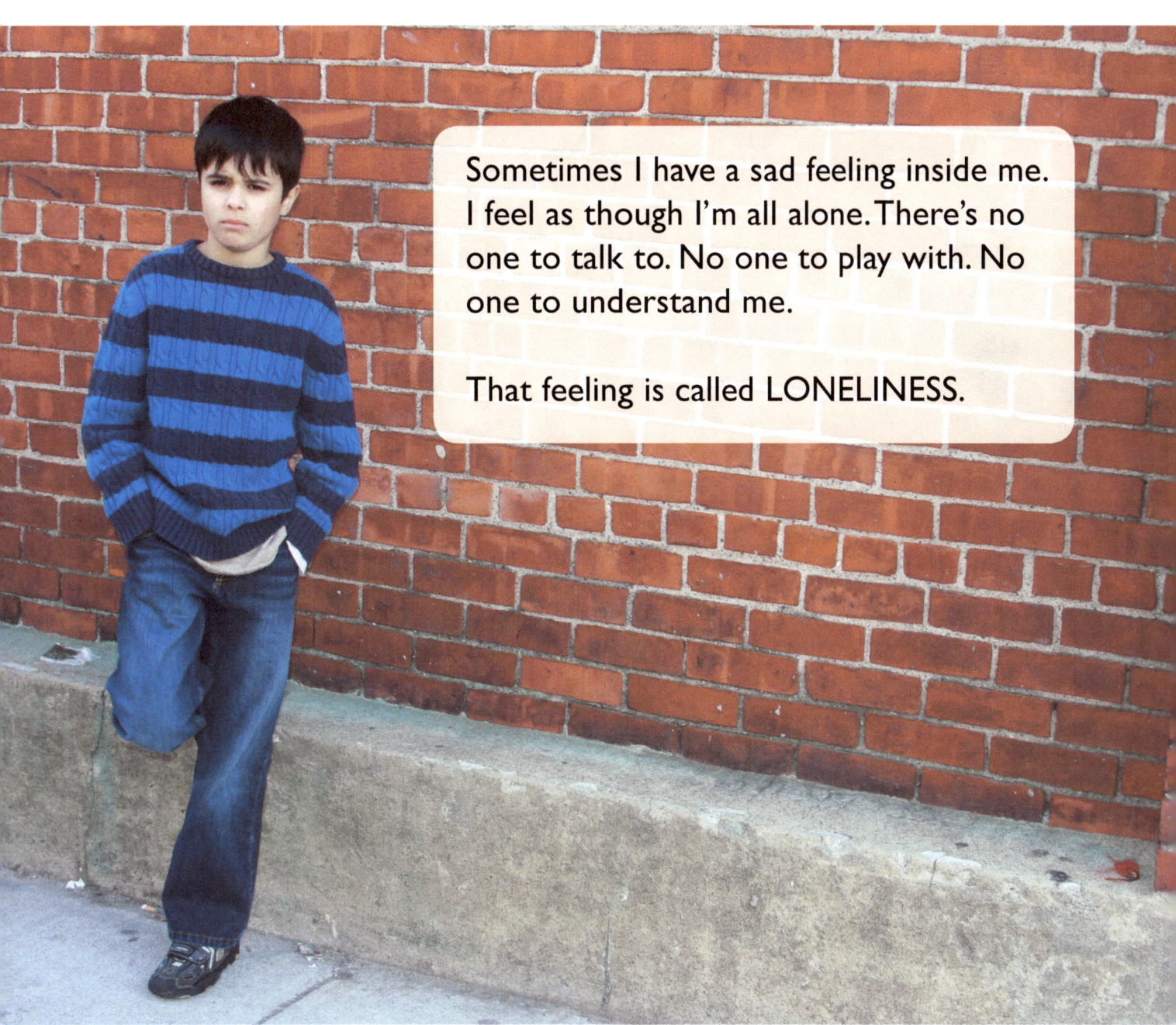

Sometimes I have a sad feeling inside me. I feel as though I'm all alone. There's no one to talk to. No one to play with. No one to understand me.

That feeling is called LONELINESS.

Loneliness is just one of the feelings I have sometimes. It doesn't last forever. Sooner or later, I feel something else instead. Even though I feel lonely today, I might wake up tomorrow feeling happy.

Or I might feel lonely this morning, but later on today, I could be so surprised that I forget all about being lonely!

One minute I could be feeling lonely—and the next minute, I'm feeling silly. The silliness pushes the loneliness right out of me!

Or I might get so angry that my loneliness goes away.

That's the thing about feelings like these—they don't last forever. These feelings come from what's going on around me, and that's always changing. There's always something new happening that gives me a new feeling inside.

When you count up all the money you've saved in your piggy bank, you might feel proud.

You might feel happy when you're doing something fun, like finger painting.

You feel surprised when someone gives you a present you weren't expecting!

Lots of times our feelings come from things happening with the people around us. You might feel angry when you have a fight with your sister.

Maybe you feel sad and worried when your parents argue.

Or you could feel sorry and guilty when your grandpa scolds you.

Another name for all those different feelings is EMOTIONS. Emotions are the feelings that come and go inside us.

All emotions are normal. Everyone feels lonely sometimes, just like everyone feels happy, sad, angry, and scared sometimes. Emotions that feel good don't make you a better person—and the emotions that hurt don't make you a bad person!

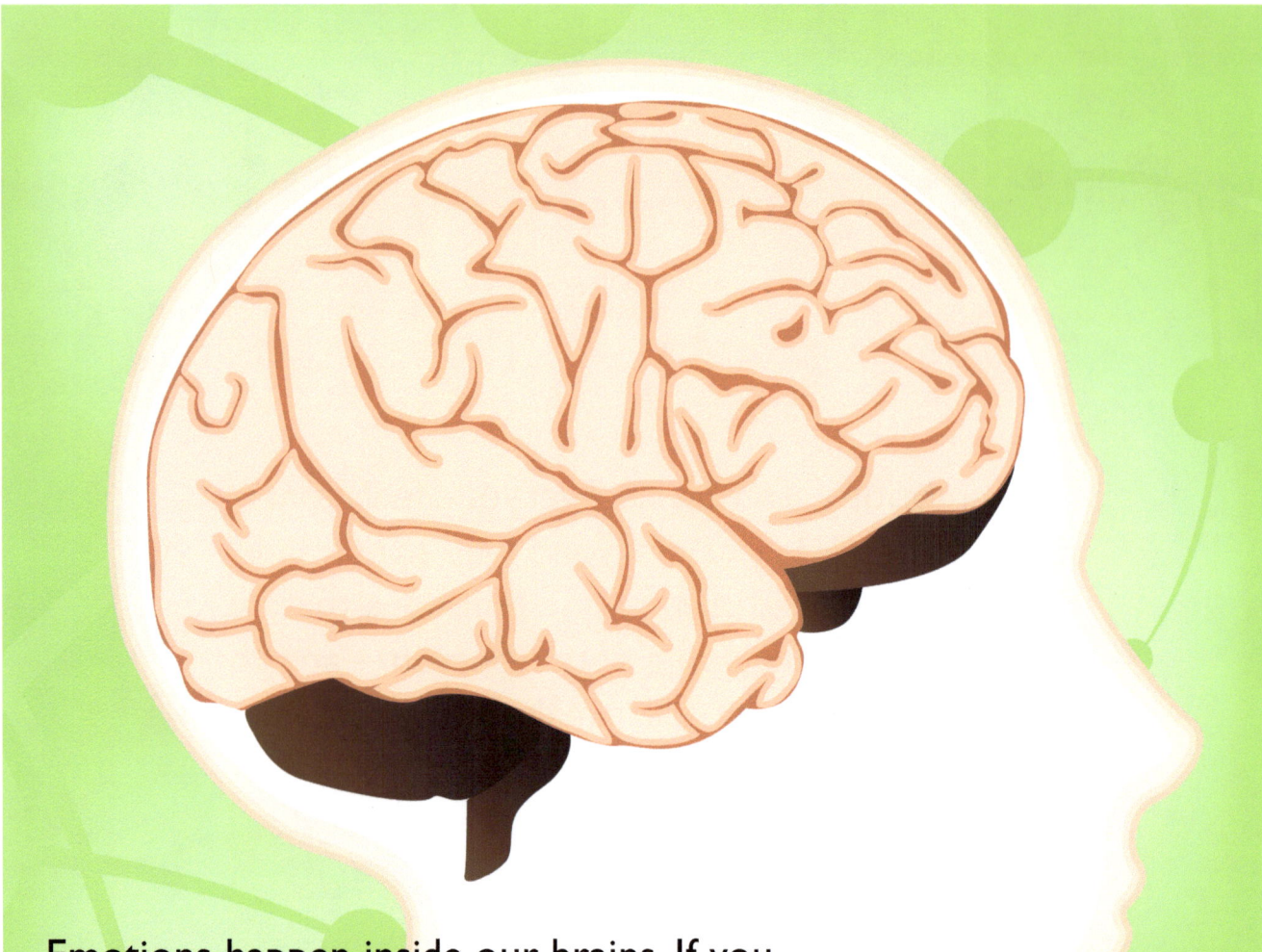

Emotions happen inside our brains. If you could look inside your head, you would see a big wrinkly thing that takes up all the space inside your skull. (Your skull is the bone inside your head.) That big wrinkly thing is your brain!

REMEMBER

HUNGRY

Your brain does amazing things. It learns new things. It thinks of ideas. It tells your body to run and play, scratch your nose, eat dinner, or go to sleep. And it makes you feel things like loneliness and happiness and worry. When something happens OUTSIDE you, your brain makes one of the feelings we call emotions INSIDE you.

SAD

IDEA!

RUN

HAPPY

DREAM

When there's no one to play with me at the beach, sometimes I feel lonely.

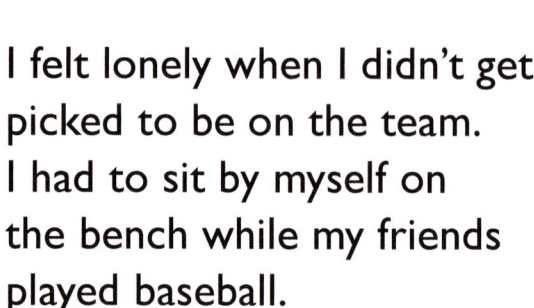

I felt lonely when I didn't get picked to be on the team. I had to sit by myself on the bench while my friends played baseball.

When my family doesn't understand me, I feel lonely.

When I got lost in the city, I felt so lonely I was scared. I didn't know where my dad was, and I didn't know how to get home. I curled up and cried.

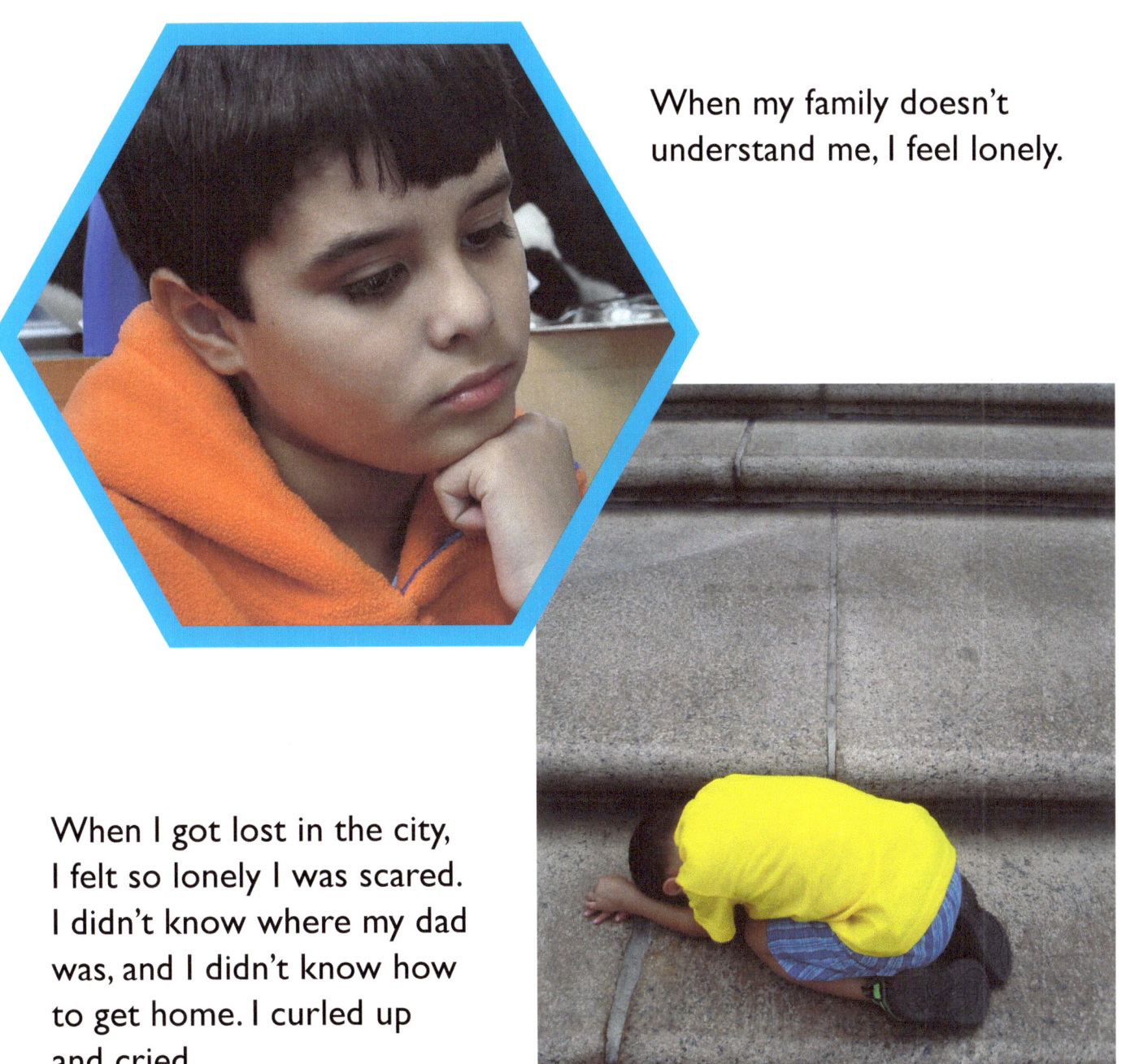

But just being alone, by myself, doesn't ALWAYS make me lonely. The funny thing is—sometimes I LIKE to be alone!

Yesterday, I had fun on my skateboard all by myself. Being alone helped me concentrate. I practiced over and over—and then I got better and better.

The first time I walked home from school all by myself, without my brother, I felt proud. I didn't feel lonely at all!

Sometimes I like to sit on my special rock in the park, all by myself. I pretend and make up stories in my head. Being alone then makes me happy.

Other times, I like to be alone at the beach. I look out at the ocean, and I think about things. Being alone gives me a chance to figure out my problems.

So I guess being lonely isn't so much about actually being alone. It's more about feeling as though I need other people when they're not there. Or they're there, but they don't understand me.

Different things make different people feel lonely. Going to a new school might make you lonely.

Being picked on or bullied can make you lonely too.

If your parents decide they're not going to live together anymore, you might feel lonely. They still love you, but you miss not being with them both.

Having to say good-bye to your best friend when her family moves to a new town could make you lonely.

When you're sick, you might feel lonely lying in bed. Everyone else is busy, except you. This kind of loneliness could feel a little like being bored. There's no one around to talk to, and there's nothing to do. You just have to lie there and feel sick!

When someone you love dies, that can be one of the loneliest feelings of all.

Everyone has these lonely feelings sometimes. Even grownups feel lonely! They feel lonely for pretty much the same reasons kids do.

A grownup might be lonely because there's no one to talk to and nothing to do.

Being sick and in the hospital can make a grownup feel lonely.

When someone's children are all grown, and the people he loves have died, a grownup can feel sad and very lonely.

A grownup who is worried about a big problem may feel lonely too.

Being lonely doesn't need to mean you're all alone. Both grownups and kids can feel lonely even when they're with lots of people. They might feel lonely because they feel different from everyone else!

Grownups aren't so different from kids! They have all the same emotions kids do. They feel happy and sad, scared and angry. Lots of times, feeling lonely can go along with other emotions. People can be lonely and scared. They might be lonely and sad. Or lonely and bored. Or lonely and worried.

Sometimes I can tell when grownups are feeling lonely by paying attention to their faces. The shape of their eyes and their mouths tell me what they're feeling. Even if they don't talk to me about their emotions, their faces give me clues about what they're feeling inside.

My face tells people when I'm feeling lonely too. So does my body. I might put my head down when I'm lonely.

The corners of my mouth could turn down instead of up.

My shoulders might slump down.

My eyebrows might go lower when I'm lonely.

All these things tell people how I'm feeling without me ever saying a word!

Even though my face and body tell people I'm lonely, it's still a good idea to talk about my feelings.

When I tell my dad I'm feeling lonely, he can help me by giving me a hug. Then I don't feel so alone.

Or my dad might make me laugh. It's hard to laugh and feel lonely at the same time!

If he knows I'm feeling lonely, my dad might do something fun with my brother and me.

If I tell my big brother I'm feeling lonely, he might be extra nice to me to cheer me up!

Everyone feels lonely sometimes, but loneliness shouldn't last a long time. If it does, you might need someone to help you. Too much loneliness can make you feel sick. It can make you feel sad all the time. You should tell a grownup what you're feeling.

Tell your mom or dad. Tell your teacher or someone else at school. Talk to someone at your church, synagogue, or mosque. Or talk to your doctor. When you let one of these grownups know how lonely you feel, they can help.

Everyone has emotions—but sometimes, everyone needs a little help with their feelings. It's okay to ask for help if your loneliness doesn't go away!

When I feel worried, the grownups in my life can help me feel better. But there are also things I can do all by myself to make the loneliness go away. I might still be alone—but I won't feel as lonely.

Being with an animal makes me feel less lonely.

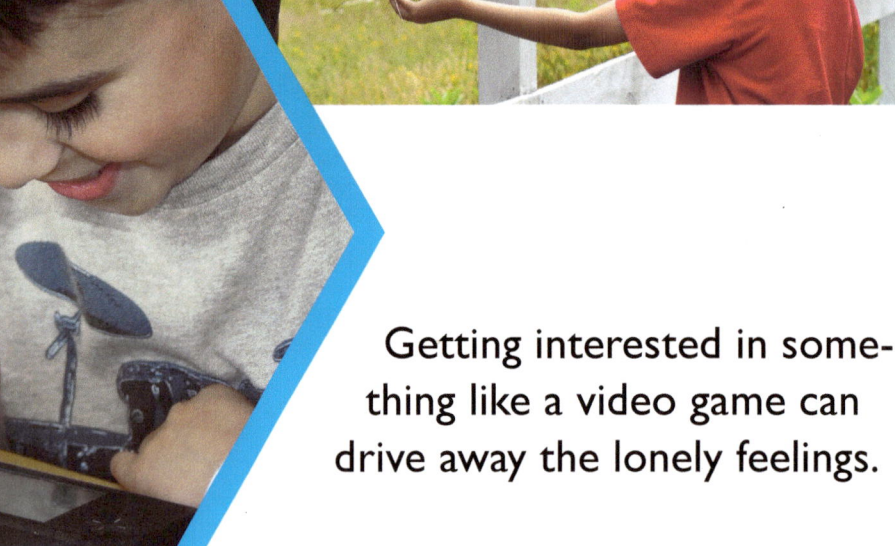

Getting interested in something like a video game can drive away the lonely feelings.

Making pictures is a good way to handle loneliness. And so is making music! I don't have to be good at drawing or playing an instrument. Just making something always helps me feel better.

I can help other people feel better too when they're lonely. If I pay attention to my brother's face, I can tell when he is feeling lonely.

Then I can do something to make him smile, so he won't feel sad anymore.

When I see one of my friends looking lonely, I can ask him to play with me.

When I see my mom wearing a lonely face, I can give her a hug.

I can spend time with my grandma and make her smile. Then she won't feel so lonely.

Being lonely doesn't feel good. But it's like a little nudge that pushes me toward other people. It makes me remember to reach out to others. It reminds me how much I need my family and my friends.

And there's a funny thing. The best way to stop feeling lonely is to help someone else! When I care how my friend is feeling and try to help him, I don't feel lonely anymore. It feels good to know I can help someone feel better. My loneliness disappears.

Try it out! See if it works for you.

Find Out More

You can learn more about your emotions by going online and checking out these websites. Some of the sites have videos you can watch or games you can play. You could also read the other books in this series to find out more about feelings—or you could go to your library and see if you can find the books listed on the next page. There's a lot more you can learn about loneliness and other feelings!

On the Internet

It's My Life: Emotions
pbskids.org/itsmylife/emotions

KidsHealth: Feelings
kidshealth.org/kid/feeling

Model Me: Faces and Emotions
www.modelmekids.com/emotions_dvd.html

In Books

Bernheimer, Kate. *The Lonely Book*. New York: Random House, 2012.

Cutler, Dave. *When I Wished I Was Alone*. Pine Bush, NY: GreyCore Press, 2003.

Harris, Isobel. *Little Boy Brown*. New York: Enchanted Lion Books, 2013.

Kim, Young-Ah. *Some Days Are Lonely*. Washington, DC: Magination Press, 2013.

Thompson, Carl. *The Big Little Book of Happy Sadness*. La Jolla, CA: Kane/Miller, 2008.

Viorst, Judith. *Nobody Here but Me*. New York: Farrar, Straus & Giroux, 2008.

Feeling Words

Lonely is just one of the words we use when we talk about feelings. But there are many more words that describe feelings. Here are some of those words.

Excited

Angry

Embarrassed

Worried

Guilty

Hurt

Proud

Scared

Shy

Sorry

Surprised

Bored

Index

An index is a way you can quickly find something inside a book. The numbers tell you exactly what page to go to if you want to find that word.

angry 11, 13, 15, 28
animal 36

body 17, 30, 32
bored 25, 28
brain 16–17
brother 20, 33, 38

church 35

dad 19, 32–33, 35
different 14, 24, 27–28
doctor 35

emotion 14–17, 28–29, 35
eyebrows 31
eyes 29

face 29–30, 32, 38–39

family 19, 25, 40
friend 18, 25, 38, 40–41
fun 12, 20, 33

game 36
grandma 39
grownups 26–29, 34–36
guilty 13

happy 10, 12, 15, 17, 21, 28
hug 32, 39

laugh 32

mom 35, 39
mosque 35
mouth 29–30
music 37

parents 13, 24
picture 37
problem 21, 27
proud 12, 20

sad 9, 13, 15, 17, 27–28, 34, 38
scared 15, 19, 28
shoulder 31
sick 25–26, 34
silly 11
sister 13
skull 16
sorry 13
surprise 10, 12
synagogue 35

teacher 35

worried 13, 27–28, 36

Picture Credits

p. 9: © Canettistock | Dreamstime.com
p. 10: © Canettistock | Dreamstime.com
p. 11: © Canettistock | Dreamstime.com
p. 12: © Katrina Brown | Dreamstime.com, © Francesco Carucci | Dreamstime.com, © Wavebreakmedia Ltd. | Dreamstime.com
p. 13: © Tiziana Casalta | Dreamstime.com, © Wavebreakmedia Ltd. | Dreamstime.com, © Ljupco Smokovski | Dreamstime.com
p. 14–15: © Beatwalk | Dreamstime.com
p. 16: © Gregory Dyer | Dreamstime.com
p. 17: © Duel964 | Dreamstime.com
p. 18: © Canettistock | Dreamstime.com
p. 19: © Canettistock | Dreamstime.com
p. 20: © Canettistock | Dreamstime.com
p. 21: © Canettistock | Dreamstime.com
p. 22–23: © Canettistock | Dreamstime.com
p. 24: © Zurijeta | Dreamstime.com, © Godfer | Dreamstime.com, Emese73 | Dreamstime.com
p. 25: © R Eko Bintoro | Dreamstime.com, © Panco971 | Dreamstime.com, © Marcel De Grijs | Dreamstime.com
p. 26: © Monkey Business Images Ltd. | Dreamstime.com, © R Eko Bintoro | Dreamstime.com
p. 27: © Anna Lurye | Dreamstime.com, © Kmira Gaya | Dreamstime.com, © C. Claudia | Dreamstime.com
p. 28–29 © Bowie15 | Dreamstime.com
p. 30: © Canettistock | Dreamstime.com
p. 31: © Canettistock | Dreamstime.com
p. 32: © Canettistock | Dreamstime.com
p. 33: © Canettistock | Dreamstime.com
p. 34: © Dbirdinparadise | Dreamstime.com, © Marsia16 | Dreamstime.com, © Nikolay Mamluke | Dreamstime.com, © Raycan | Dreamstime.com
p. 35: © Elena Kouptsova-vasic | Dreamstime.com, © George Muresan | Dreamstime.com, © Monkey Business Images Ltd. | Dreamstime.com
p. 36: © Canettistock | Dreamstime.com, © Renomartin | Dreamstime.com
p. 37: © Canettistock | Dreamstime.com
p. 38: © Canettistock | Dreamstime.com, © Yelena Rodriguez | Dreamstime.com,
p. 39: © Laurley | Dreamstime.com, © Canettistock | Dreamstime.com
p. 40: © Canettistock | Dreamstime.com, © Zurijeta | Dreamstime.com
p. 41: © Canettistock | Dreamstime.com
p. 44: Fotolia: © Fasphotographic, © Cantor Pannato, © Andres Rodriguez, © Gabriel Blaj, © Moodboard Premium, © Halfpoint
p. 45: Fotolia: © Cantor Pannato, © Blend Images, © Zhekos, © Olly, © Wavebreak Media Micro; © Serrnovik | Dreamstime.com

About the Author

Alexandra Dalton was a teacher, and now she is a writer. When she was a teacher, she helped her students talk about their feelings. She knows that it's hard work sometimes to talk about our feelings—but she knows we feel better and we get along with each other better when we can use our words to talk about how we feel. Alexandra has three children. She also has a dog and a cat and four goats. She lives in New York State.

www.ingramcontent.com/pod-product-compliance
Lightning Source LLC
Chambersburg PA
CBHW061359090426
42743CB00002B/69